Two Babies in a Manger

Written by **Dr. Cheryl Lentz**

Illustrated by **Karen Light**

Narratore Press

GRAYSLAKE, ILLINOIS

Published by
Narratore Press
www.NarratorePress.com

Books are available through Narratore Press at special discounts for bulk purchases for the purpose of sales promotion, seminar attendance, or educational purposes.

Two Babies in a Manger is based on a story that appears to be folklore.

Illustrations by Karen Light
Production by Gary Rosenberg
Narratore Press Logo by Dr. Natalie Casale

A special thank you to Dr. Valerie Weber, Melody Johnson,
and Lois Mcquire for their reviews.

About the Author

Known as the Academic Entrepreneur, **Dr. Cheryl Lentz** is a unique and dynamic speaker who connects intensely with her audience, having one foot in academia and one foot in the business and entrepreneurial space.

Known globally for her writings on leadership and failure, as well as critical and refractive thinking, Dr. Cheryl has been published more than 44 times with 25 writing awards. As an accomplished university professor, speaker, and consultant, she is an international best-selling author and top-quoted publishing professional on ABC, CBS, NBC, and Fox. She takes the stage as a TEDx speaker in *Farmingdale2020, October 10, 2020.

Please visit www.DrCherylLentz.com
www.facebook.com/Dr.Cheryl.Lentz
www.linkedin.com/in/drcheryllentz/
www.youtube.com/drcheryllentz
www.instagram.com/drcheryllentz/
or e-mail: drcheryllentz@gmail.com

Follow your heart and you'll never get lost.

This book is a gift for

Author's Note

During the Christmas Eve service in 2019 at my local church, I heard a new version of the traditional Christmas story during the sermon. Tears rolled down my face as my heart connected with the true meaning of Christmas as seen through the eyes of a young orphan. I related my experience at holiday gatherings many times in the days that followed, and everyone seemed to have a similar reaction to mine. As a writer, I felt compelled to create this children's book to share the magic of the story with you.

Moved by this tale in a way as no other, I went in search of the author. My search led to many links on the Internet, but my attempts at finding its owner were ultimately unsuccessful. The story seems to be common folklore known by some, repeated by many, but without established genesis. If you know the original storyteller, please share with us so that we may give appropriate credit.

In a world of tragedy and sorrow, this version of the Christmas story will renew your faith in humanity through the words of a young orphan boy who discovers the true meaning of Christmas and family. In his search for a forever home, Ben realizes that home is the gift you offer from your heart—and it is in that giving we connect with the true meaning of finding the love of our forever family.

Enjoy this amazing journey in the retelling of the traditional Christmas story with a unique ending that will truly touch your heart as you discover new meaning of the joys of the season. Keep the tissues nearby . . .

Merry Christmas—from my family to yours.   *Dr. Cheryl*

2

Hi. My name is Benigno. My friends call me Ben.

I'm 8 years old. I live in a foster home. This is a place that takes care of kids who don't have a family or anyone to take care of them.

I live here with other boys and girls who don't have a mom or dad either.

We live together with Annabelle and Jacob. They take care of us like a mom and dad.

We take care of each other until we find our forever family.

Today we have a visitor.

3

"Hi, I'm Father Tom. I am from the Church of the Sacred Heart nearby. I am here to share a story of two people who needed a place to stay and received an amazing gift. This is the story of the birth of Jesus Christ. It is the holiday we all know as Christmas!"

God sent an angel to a young girl named Mary, who told her that she would have a baby who would be God's Son, Jesus. He would save people from their sins.

Months later, It was time for Mary to have her baby. Mary and her husband Joseph traveled to the city of Bethlehem. They tried to find a place to stay but all the rooms were already rented for the night.

A kind innkeeper offered his barn. Mary and Joseph accepted. Mary then gave birth to Jesus, wrapped Him in a blanket, and laid Him in the manger. Baby Jesus was the best gift of all. They were surrounded by little lambs, donkeys, and other animals that welcomed Him.

A bright star shone in the sky that night—the Star of Bethlehem.

The children hung on every word in wonder about this special family—Mary, Joseph, and baby Jesus.

Father Tom continued:

"People from near and far travelled to see the baby Jesus. Three wise men followed the star looking for the newborn King, bringing gifts of gold, perfume, and other spices."

As Father Tom finished reading, Ben was smiling—and even seemed a bit happier than before the story started.

Annabelle said to Father Tom, "Thank you so much for coming to our home and reading that special Christmas story. What do we say kids?"

Everyone said in unison, "Thank you!"

Father Tom smiled and said, "You're welcome! I also have something else for you! We are going to make our own manger scene."

After the story, Father Tom brought gifts for the children, giving them many things to make their own manger scene.

While the children were busy making their mangers, Father Tom visited with each child.

When Father Tom came to Ben's table, however, he noticed that Ben had not one but two babies in his manger.

Curious, Father Tom asked Ben, "Why are there two babies in your manger, Ben?"

Ben very slowly and very seriously began to repeat the story that Father Tom told them. Ben had only heard the Christmas story for the first time, but he repeated nearly every word perfectly—until he came to the part where Mary laid baby Jesus in the manger.

Then Ben added a surprise ending. Father Tom listened intently to Ben's unexpected words.

"The story of Jesus . . . it made me feel good. Like in my heart."

Ben then repeated the entire Christmas story. He beamed at Father Tom and said:

"I smiled and talked with Jesus as He was in the manger. He smiled back at me, and asked ME if I also had a place to stay."

Sadly, Ben told Him no.

Father Tom felt the young boy's pain.
Then Ben's eyes got big.

"Jesus told me I could stay with Him!"

16

"But I told Him I couldn't. I didn't have a gift to give Him, like the wise men did in the story.

"But I wanted to stay with Jesus so much. I thought about what I had to give Him as a gift."

Ben wiped away his tears and continued.

"I asked Jesus if I could stay with Him—but I had nothing to give as a gift. Then I remembered my warm coat. He had only a cloth on his body.

"I asked Him if I could give Him a gift I have on me—the gift of being warm.

"And Jesus smiled and said, 'If you keep me warm, that will be the best gift anybody could ever give me.'"

"So I climbed into the manger and wrapped my arms around Jesus to keep Him warm."

"*Then Jesus smiled and told me I could stay with Him forever.*"

Father Tom was amazed at Ben's wisdom as he retold the Christmas story.

24

Ben had learned the most important lesson of all. He finally found his forever home with baby Jesus and the Holy Family—a family who would never leave him, a family who would love him and stay with him forever.

CPSIA information can be obtained at www.ICGtesting.com
Printed in the USA
BVIW121333121020
590819BV00007B/10